Nature's Children

ZEBRAS

Bill Ivy

GROLIER
EDUCATIONAL

FACTS IN BRIEF

Classification of Zebras

Class:	*Mammalia* (mammals)
Order:	*Perissodactyla* (odd-toed ungulates)
Family:	*Equidae* (horse family)
Genus:	*Equus*
Species:	*Equus quagga* (Plains Zebra);
	Equus greyvi (Grevy's Zebra);
	Equus zebra (Mountain Zebra).

World distribution.   Africa.

Habitat.   Varies with species.

Distinctive physical characteristics.   Black and white striped coat, the pattern of which varies with the species.

Habits.   Plains and Mountain zebras live in rigidly structured bands; the Grevy's Zebra tends to be solitary, though temporary groups may form.

Diet.   Zebras eat only plants, mainly grasses, shrubs and herbs.

**Published originally as
"Getting to Know . . . Nature's Children."**

This series is approved and recommended by the Federation of Ontario Naturalists.

This library reinforced edition is available exclusively from:

GROLIER
EDUCATIONAL

Sherman Turnpike, Danbury, Connecticut 06816

Contents

If you were asked to name a word that starts with the letter Z, what word would you pick? Chances are it would be zebra.

Few animals in the world are as well known as the zebra. In fact, it has even found its way into some common expressions. Can you think of one? Perhaps you have heard people say "a zebra can't change its stripes." They mean that you can't be something you are not. Another common expression, "a horse of a different color," was once used to describe the zebra. Today it means anything unique or different. That is certainly true of zebras. They are fascinating animals whose life story is filled with adventure, danger and fun.

The early Greeks called zebras "horse-tigers."

Horse

Zebra

What's the Difference?

How would you describe a zebra? A horse with stripes? Well, things are not always as black and white as they may seem! While horses and zebras are very similar in many ways, there are differences.

Zebras are not as tall as most horses, for one thing. And zebras have shorter, more erect manes and smaller, narrower hoofs. Their ears are larger than those of horses as well, and their tails are quite different. Zebras have long tails with short hair tufts at the tip, while a horse's tail is covered with long and flowing hair. Also, unlike horses, some zebras have a fold of skin, known as a dewlap, under their throats. And some zebras lack "chestnuts," those callous growths often found on a horse's inner leg.

Finally, there's one other big difference: unlike horses, which are mainly domesticated, zebras are wild and cannot be trained.

Zebra Relatives

It is easy to tell by looking that the zebra is a member of the horse family. The scientific name for this family is *Equidae* and it includes not only horses and zebras, but also donkeys and wild asses. Several of the zebra's relatives live in Asia and Africa. Let's take a look at some of them.

The ancestor of all domestic horses is the wild Przewalski's horse, which once ranged in central Asia but is now found only in zoos and reserves. Like the zebra, it has a mane that stands straight up. Wild asses are found in Africa and Asia. The African ass, the ancestor of the familiar domestic donkey, is very rare in the wild. There are several Asiatic wild asses. In general they are larger than the African species and more horse-like. The largest of all is the kiang, which can still be found in fairly large numbers in certain areas of Tibet.

The Przewalski's horse.

Curious Coat

There is certainly no mistaking a zebra with its black and white patterned coat. Take a look at the zebra on this page and try to solve this puzzle: is the zebra white with black stripes or black with white stripes? Most people think that zebras are white, since you can barely see the faint dark stripes on some animals. In some parts of Africa there are even zebras with spots instead of stripes on their hindquarters!

Surprisingly, not all zebras are just black and white. They may have brown, gray, yellow or buff-colored stripes. Often there are lighter bands, called shadow stripes, between the darker ones. But whatever the design, no two zebras are exactly alike. Their striped patterns are as individual as your fingerprints.

Bewildering Bands

The zebra's striped coat is certainly striking, but it is also useful. It helps the zebra hide from its enemies. A zebra's enemies see the world differently than we do. Just as we cannot distinguish color outside by moonlight (try it tonight, you'll see what I mean), many animals cannot see color at all, even in bright daylight. They see their world only in black and white and shades of gray. For this reason, the zebra's stripes make it less noticeable because they don't stick out against the background.

But that's not all. The zebra's striped coat also breaks up the animal's outline, making it very hard to see from far away. And when a herd of zebras group together, it is almost impossible to tell where one ends and another begins. This form of camouflage works very well!

How many zebras can you see in this picture?

Horse Sense

Zebras have razor-sharp senses—and a good thing too, because they must always be on the lookout for danger.

A zebra has excellent eyesight and can see much farther into the distance than we can. It can also focus up close and far away at the same time. How? The pupils of a zebra's eyes are not round like ours, but oblong. So when a zebra is feeding, it can focus on the grass with one part of its eye and look out for danger with the other part. (Try to do that yourself and you will instantly go cross-eyed!)

The zebra's other senses are also very important for its survival. Many times it will smell danger before actually seeing it, and its cup-shaped ears turn in all directions to funnel in sounds. In fact, zebras have such good hearing, it is almost impossible to sneak up on one!

The zebra's eyes are set well back on its head, enabling it to see all around.

Born to Run

The zebra is a superb runner. Its strong heart and lungs and its muscular legs let it bolt away with incredible speed. Zebras have been clocked at 100 kilometres (60 miles) per hour. That is as fast as a car speeding down a highway! While it cannot keep up this pace for long, a zebra can run as fast as a car driving down a city street for 25 kilometres (15 miles) or so.

Most of the time, however, a zebra's pace of life is not that hectic. Like a horse, it has three speeds, or gaits: walking, trotting and galloping. Usually it moves at an easy walk.

Whether it is moving fast or slowly, only one toe of each of the zebra's feet touches the ground. That's the fully developed middle toe, which is surrounded by a hard protective covering, or hoof.

Beating the Itch

Have you heard this joke:

Question: What's black and white and red
all over?

Answer: A sunburnt zebra, of course!

While the idea of a zebra with a sunburn is rather silly, too much sun *can* be harmful. The sun and hot winds can dry out a zebra's skin and make it itchy. In order to scratch itself, a zebra rubs against tree stumps, rocks and even its friends. To get at those hard to reach spots, it lies down and rolls on the ground. This feels good and covers the zebra with dirt and mud that help to protect it from the heat and wind.

Often a zebra is also bothered by tiny insects that burrow into its hide. This is where teamwork comes in handy. Zebras often nibble each other's backs to get rid of those itchy pests. This mutual grooming also acts as a soothing massage. After all, who doesn't like back rubs? Another solution is to take a bath—a dust bath, that is. Not the best way to keep clean perhaps, but it does help the zebra stay pest free.

Opposite page:
Once a good spot for a dust bath is found, several zebras may take turns using it.

Coarse Cuisine

Zebras never hunt. They feed only on plants. Their favorites are grasses, shrubs and herbs, but they will eat any available bulbs and fruits. Much of this food is very coarse. If we ate zebra food regularly, our teeth would quickly wear down. However, zebras have special teeth that are sunk deep into their jaws and grow throughout their lives. When one of a zebra's teeth wears down, just the right amount of tooth pushes up out of the jaw to replace what has worn away. Also, by chewing sideways, the zebra keeps the grinding edges of its teeth sharp.

Zebras spend as much as half of each day grazing. Most zebras must also drink daily. If there is not enough food or water available, they may travel up to 45 kilometres (30 miles) a day to satisfy their hunger and thirst.

Grazing in the grass.

On the Alert

A zebra's life is full of danger. Lions are its greatest enemy, although jackals, wild dogs and hyenas are also a threat. However, a zebra is not an easy prey because it is very cautious. Usually only the weak, sick or careless become the victims of a hungry predator.

Zebras know there is safety in numbers. When a herd is feeding or drinking, one zebra stands guard and warns the herd at the first sign of danger. At night, a male stallion stands guard. If an enemy attacks, the night watchman sounds the alarm. While the rest of the herd flees, he stays behind to face the attacker.

Zebras have another easy way of keeping watch. When two zebras stand side by side they face in opposite directions. That way they can keep alert for any surprise attacks.

Zebras are incredibly loyal. If a mare and her young are in trouble, a group of stallions will come to their rescue. If a member of the herd is injured or sick, the rest of the group may slow down to its pace. The elderly are also helped along and are even brought food.

Opposite page:
For added protection, zebras often gather around giraffes because they make such excellent watchtowers.

Meet the Family

If you want to see zebras in the wild, you will have to visit Africa. That is now their only home, although scientists believe they once lived in Europe.

There are three different species of zebras and they live in different parts of Africa. However, there is some overlap and, in certain areas, two types can be seen together.

The Plains Zebra is found in the savannah and grassland areas of the central and eastern flatlands. The Grevy's Zebra, sometimes called the desert zebra, lives in the low hill country. The Mountain Zebra inhabits rocky stretches of land in the southern part of Africa.

Plains Zebra
Grevy's Zebra
Mountain Zebra

Opposite page:
The handsome Grevy's Zebra is basically a loner.

The shaded areas on this map show where zebras live in Africa.

The Plains Zebra

The Plains Zebra (often called Burchell's Zebra) is still found in herds as large as 10 000. Most are fat-looking animals with short legs. Their stripe pattern varies from place to place: the farther south they live, the less prominent their stripes. All Plains Zebras have a black muzzle and a tail with a rather long tassel.

The Plains Zebra is the one you are most likely to get a chance to see for yourself— without going to Africa. It is the kind most often found in zoos.

The Plains Zebra has been described as rather dumpy. What do you think?

The Mountain Zebra

The Mountain Zebra is the smallest of all
zebras. It has a brown muzzle, long tapered
ears, a short tail tuft and a dewlap. Living
together in small herds of about six animals,
Mountain Zebras keep to themselves. However,
if food is plentiful, they will group together in
large numbers. Mountain Zebras can go for
longer periods without water than their cousin,
the Plains Zebra.

With its streamlined body, thin legs and
narrow hoofs, the Mountain Zebra is well suited
for its life in the hills. As you might expect, it is
an excellent climber and can scale steep rocky
cliffs with ease. Mountain Zebras are creatures
of habit. They like to follow the same well-worn
paths. These handsome animals are not very
common, but fortunately they are protected in
Africa's national parks.

Mountain Zebras.

The Grevy's Zebra

There is no mistaking the Grevy's Zebra. Standing over a metre and a half (5 feet) at the shoulder, it is the largest of all zebras and has longer, more rounded ears than the rest of its family. Narrow stripes that run very close together line most of its body from head to hoof. Only its belly is unmarked. A single stripe runs down its back and cuts its hindquarters in two. If you were to take away a Grevy's stripes, it would look more like an ass than a horse. In fact, its voice sounds rather like a donkey's bray.

Unlike other zebras, the Grevy's likes to be alone. Many people think it is the most beautiful member of the zebra family. What do you think?

The Grevy's Zebra is the most aggressive of all the zebras.

Rank and File

Generally speaking, zebras are sociable animals. They seem to enjoy each other's company—as long as no one steps out of line. Within each band there is one male and up to six females and their young, and each member has its own distinct ranking.

The stallion is the chief. Next in importance is the senior mare. When the band is on the move, she leads the way, followed by the second-ranking mare and so on down the line to the youngest zebras. Protecting the rear is the stallion, who chases away any predators. Each member of the herd is careful to keep in line. Should any of them try to promote themselves up a position or two, look out! Their superior will promptly chase them back where they belong.

Having seniority has definite advantages. After all, the first to arrive get first dibs at the drinking hole and the pick of the choicest grasses.

Opposite page:
Young zebras are well looked after by their family.

Making Tracks

When food or water become scarce, zebras must look for "greener pastures." Africa's dry season is particularly hard on them and sometimes they are forced to travel great distances to find a meal. However, even in the driest weather, grass can usually be found along rivers and waterholes. While migrating, some species gather together in large numbers. During this time, herds containing thousands of zebras can be seen crossing the plains.

The Plains Zebra travels the farthest, migrating hundreds of kilometres (miles) each year. The Grevy's Zebra also migrates, but does not cover such a large area. Even the Mountain Zebra seeks fresh new areas to graze on, although it stays within the boundaries of the African parks and reserves where it lives.

Searching for greener pastures.

Battling Stallions

While family groups of zebras are usually easy-going, fights between stallions frequently break out. Sometimes the stallions bicker over food or territory. Often a fight will start when one tries to steal another's mare, hoping to start a family of his own.

The match usually begins with a lot of foot stomping and pushing. The combatants flatten their ears back and snort at each other. If neither backs down, the battle heats up, and they bite, kick and neck wrestle until one of them decides he has had enough. The loser surrenders by lowering his head to show that he is beaten. Although these battles are often fierce, zebras do not fight to the death.

These zebras are not just horsing around!

Zebra Talk

When you meet a friend, how do you greet each other? With a friendly hello? When two zebras meet, they greet by sniffing each other. Zebras also use their voices to communicate. Each species has its own distinctive voice. They can growl, whine, snort or whistle. There are different calls for greeting or warning one another, showing contentment or expressing pain.

Zebras also use body language. How they move their ears, tail or mouth indicates what sort of mood they are in. However, to tell if a zebra is sleeping, you may have to check if its eyes are shut because an adult zebra can sleep standing up.

The call of the Damaraland Zebra (a Plains Zebra) sounds a little like a dog's bark.

Shaky Beginnings

Zebra babies may be born at any time of the year.

When the time comes for a female zebra to give birth, she leaves the herd and begins looking for a private place. An area where the grass is not too tall is perfect. Here she delivers her baby alone. The newborn zebra, or foal, has a soft shaggy coat of brown and white stripes which its mother immediately licks clean.

Shortly after birth the wide-eyed foal struggles to its feet. This takes a bit of practice and the determined little zebra may topple over a few times before finally learning to balance on its wobbly legs. The newborn huddles close to its mother and feeds on her milk. Within an hour, the foal will be strong enough to walk or even run.

This young Plains Zebra will be independent some time around its first birthday.

Horsing Around

Once the foal is steady on its feet, the mother rejoins the herd, and it may take a few days for the foal to learn to recognize her amid the other mares.

As their youngsters sleep on the ground, the females rest nearby. At the first sign of trouble, they wake the foals and run with them to safety. Within a few weeks the foals start grazing. However, they will continue to drink their mothers' milk for at least a year.

Like all children, foals love to play. Under the watchful eyes of their mothers, they frolic and chase each other. While this "horsing around" is fun, it is also important as it helps to develop the young ones' strength and sharpens their reflexes. The adults often join in the fun and play-fight with the foals. This helps to train the youngsters for any real fights they may have in the future.

Along with fun and games, the young zebras must also learn the rules of the herd. They learn to obey their superiors and accept their ranking order.

Stepping Out

Within one to three years the young zebras will leave their families to join other herds or start one of their own. In some species, the young males, called colts, group together in bachelor clubs for a few years until they are strong and smart enough to take over or form herds of their own.

Sadly, only half of the foals born will reach adulthood. However, those that do may live for ten to twenty-five years.

In the past, zebras were hunted for their beautiful coats, but fortunately many African countries have now formed wildlife parks where zebras can roam freely, protected by the law. There is no question that these beautiful animals are worth preserving.

Words to Know

Camouflage   Colors and patterns that help an animal blend in with its surroundings.

Colt   A young male zebra.

Dewlap   A fold of loose skin hanging under the throat of some animals, including some zebras.

Foal   A baby zebra.

Gait   A particular way of walking and/or running.

Groom   Brush or clean hair or fur.

Hoofs   Hard nail-like growths that protect a zebra's feet.

Mare   A female zebra.

Migrate   To make regular journeys in search of food.

Predator   An animal that hunts other animals for food.

Reserve   An area where wildlife is protected by law.

Savannah   Flat grassland of tropical or subtropical regions.

Shadow stripes   Brownish bands found on some zebras between the dark stripes.

Stallion   A male zebra.

INDEX

Cover Photo: Boyd Norton

Photo Credits: Bill Ivy, pages 4, 8, 11, 15, 19, 31, 41; Hot Shots, pages 7, 38; Art Gryfe (Network Stock Photo File), page 12; J.P. Taylor, page 16; Boyd Norton, pages 20, 32, 34, 42; Harvey Medland (Network Stock Photo File), page 23; Metro Toronto Zoo, page 24; G.C. Kelley, page 27; B.E. Joseph (American Society of Mammologists), page 28; Four by Five Inc., page 37; E.R. Degginger, page 45.